J368 Book & CD $9.90

CELLO
SOLO BOOK 1A

the instrumental series

Richard F. Grunow
Professor of Music Education
Eastman School of Music
of the University of Rochester

Edwin E. Gordon
Research Professor
University of South Carolina

Christopher D. Azzara
Associate Professor of Music Education
Eastman School of Music
of the University of Rochester

Michael E. Martin
Instrumental Music Teacher
School District of Haverford Township
Havertown, Pennsylvania

AN INSTRUMENTAL METHOD DESIGNED FOR DEVELOPING AUDIATION SKILLS AND EXECUTIVE SKILLS

Instrument	Bk 1	CD 1	Bk1 & CD	Bk 2	CD 2	Bk 2 & CD	Solo Bk/CD 1A	Solo Bk/CD 1B	Solo Bk 2	Solo Bk 3
Violin	J318	J319	J320	J330		J332	J366	J370	J163	J218
Viola	J321	J322	J323	J333	J331	J334	J367	J371	J164	J219
Cello	J324	J325	J326	J335		J336	J368	J372	J165	J220
Bass	J327	J328	J329	J337		J338	J369	J373	J166	J221
Recorder	J231	J232	J233	J247	J245CD	J245	—	—	J149	J217

Revised Teacher's Guide for Strings Books 1 and 2	J317
Revised Teacher's Guide for Band Books 1 and 2	J315
JRI for Winds and Percussion (specify instrument)	
Revised Teacher's Guide for Recorder	J235
Solo Book 1–Writing (all instruments)	J167
Solo Book 2–Writing (all instruments)	J168
Solo Book 3–Writing (all instruments)	J203
Composition Book 1 (all instruments)	J249
GIA Heavy Duty Sporano Recorder	M447
Concert Selections for Wind and Percussion (specify instrument)	
Parent's Guide	J177

RECORDED SOLOS WITH ACCOMPANIMENTS

Cassette Bk 2: J148
Cassette Bk 3: J200
CD Bk 2: J148CD
CD Bk 3: J200CD

LISTENING

Simple Gifts	*Don Gato*	*You Are My Sunshine*
Cassette: J229CS	Cassette: J201CS	Cassette: J199CS
CD: J229CD	CD: J201CD	CD: J199CD

GIA Publications, Inc., 7404 S. Mason Ave., Chicago, IL 60638

NOTE TO STUDENTS, PARENTS, AND TEACHERS[1]

You may begin using *Solo Books 1-A and 1-B* from *Jump Right In: The Instrumental Series – for Strings* when you have learned to audiate and perform many of the songs in *Student Book One*. Exemplary performances and accompaniments for the songs in this book are recorded on the CD included inside the front cover.

Perform the songs in this book by ear before performing them from notation. First you should listen to the songs and audiate as they are performed by the professional musician on the CD that accompanies this book. Next, you should sing the songs and learn to perform them by ear on your instrument (A and B listed below – under MUSICAL ENRICHMENT ACTIVITIES).

Notice in the notation that dynamic markings, tempo markings, and stylistic markings are not indicated. Bowings are indicated; however, feel free to add slurs or make other changes. After listening to the professional musician, indicate by marking with a pencil the dynamics, tempos, bowings, and stylistic markings for each solo in the manner that it is performed on the CD. The *Music Theory* section of *Student Book Two* and *Composition Book One* provide information to help mark your music. Mark the notation with a pencil because you may decide to try musical ideas that are different from those used by the professional musician on the recording. Ask your instrumental music teacher for suggestions.

Additional MUSICAL ENRICHMENT ACTIVITIES are listed below for each song. The *Fingering Chart* in the back of this book will help you when locating unfamiliar pitches on your instrument.

You will enjoy performing all the songs in this book with your friends. When performing a few songs, however, you may wish to perform the melody an octave above or below the written melody. In some cases you may wish to perform the melody in a different keyality (start on a different note). At times, you may enjoy just listening to the performances on the CD.

Chord symbols (C, G7, Dm, etc.) are included above the music notation. You may use the chord symbols when learning to perform accompaniments, variations, and improvisations for the songs. Your instrumental music teacher will explain how to use chord symbols.

MUSICAL ENRICHMENT ACTIVITIES

A. Sing the song. You may sing the song in a different keyality (start on a different note) than found on the CD.
B. Perform the song on your instrument by ear in the same tonality and keyality that is on the CD.
C. Perform the song in a second keyality.
D. Perform the song in a third keyality.
E. Perform the song with a friend who plays the same or a different instrument.
F. Perform the song in a different meter. (For example, play duple meter tunes in triple meter and play triple meter tunes in duple meter.)
G. Perform the song in a different tonality. (For example, play major tonality songs in minor tonality, and play minor tonality songs in major tonality.)
H. Perform the bass line for the song.
I. Perform an improvisation or harmony part for the song.
J. Indicate the notation for the song. Ask your instrumental music teacher about *Solo Books – Writing*.

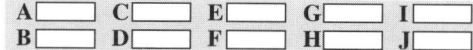

---

[1] *Solo Book 1-A/CD* (50 tunes) and *Solo Book 1-B/CD* (50 tunes) include selections chosen from the original 300 tunes released as *Solo Books One, Two, and Three*. The books and CDs feature a varied musical repertoire that follows the key sequence of instruction in *Jump Right In: The Instrumental Series – for Strings*.

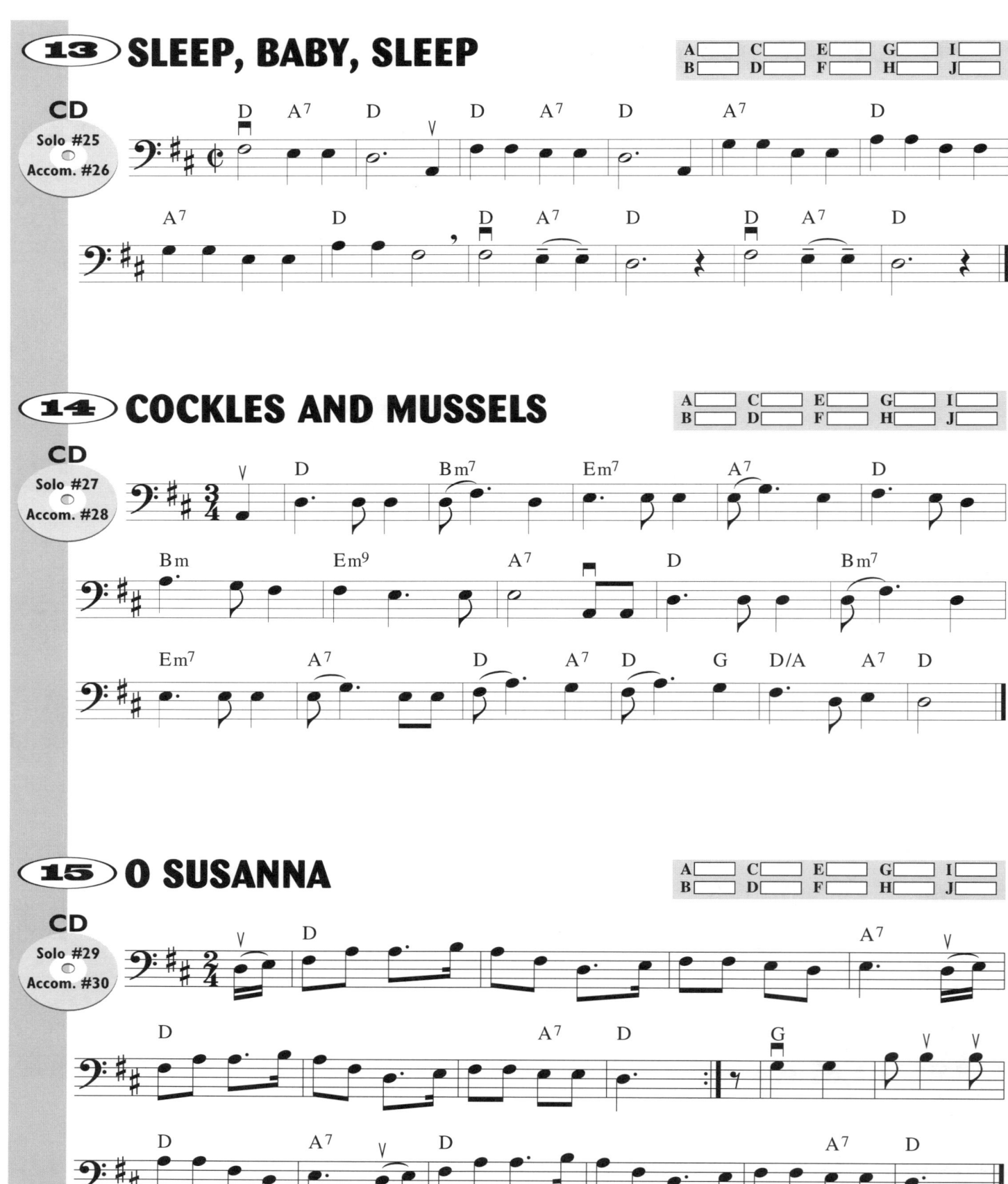

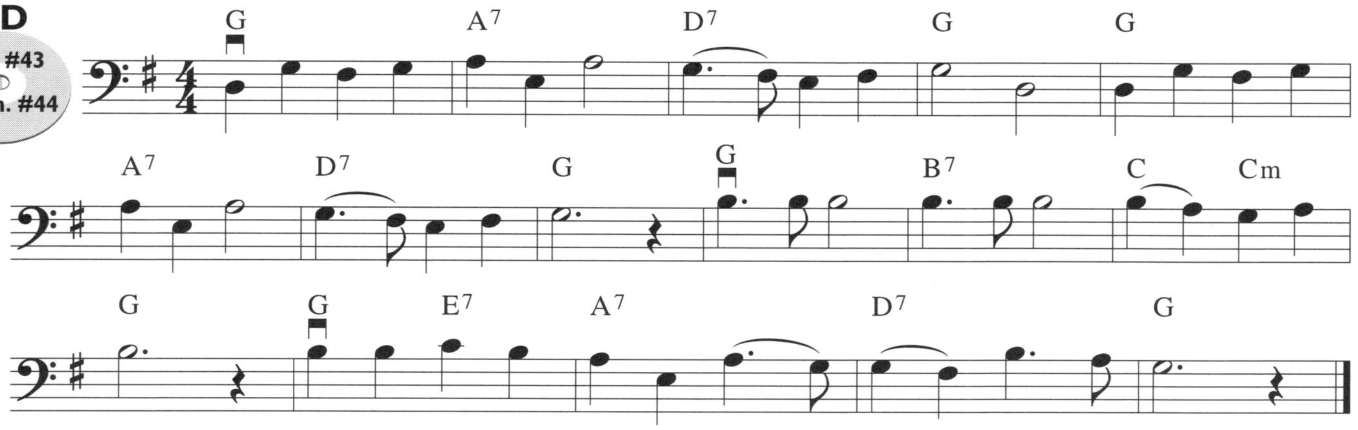

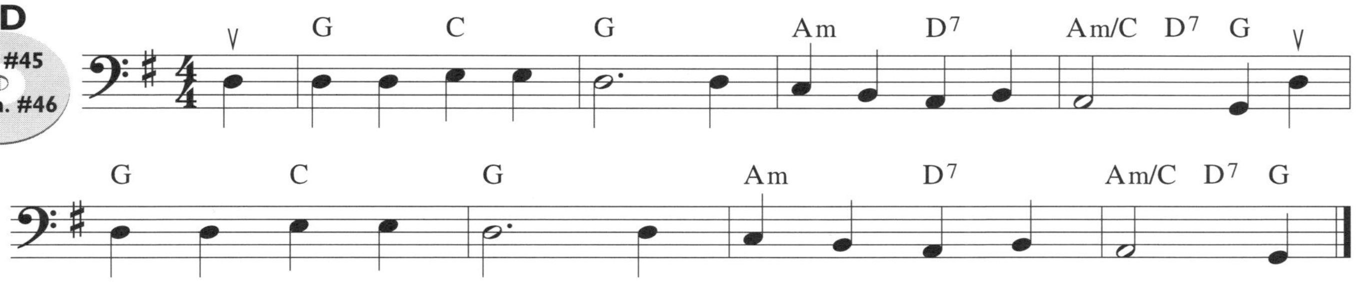

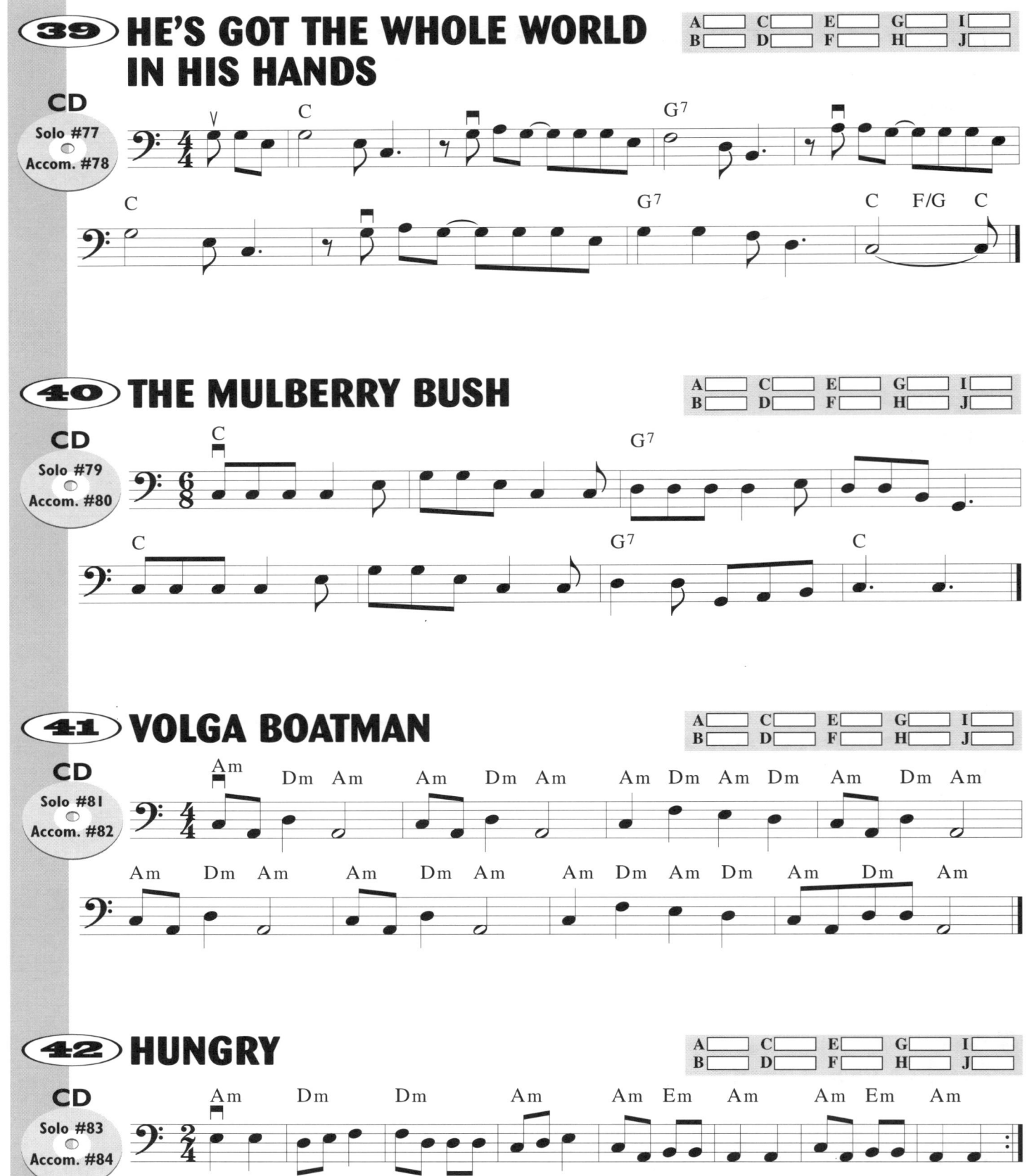

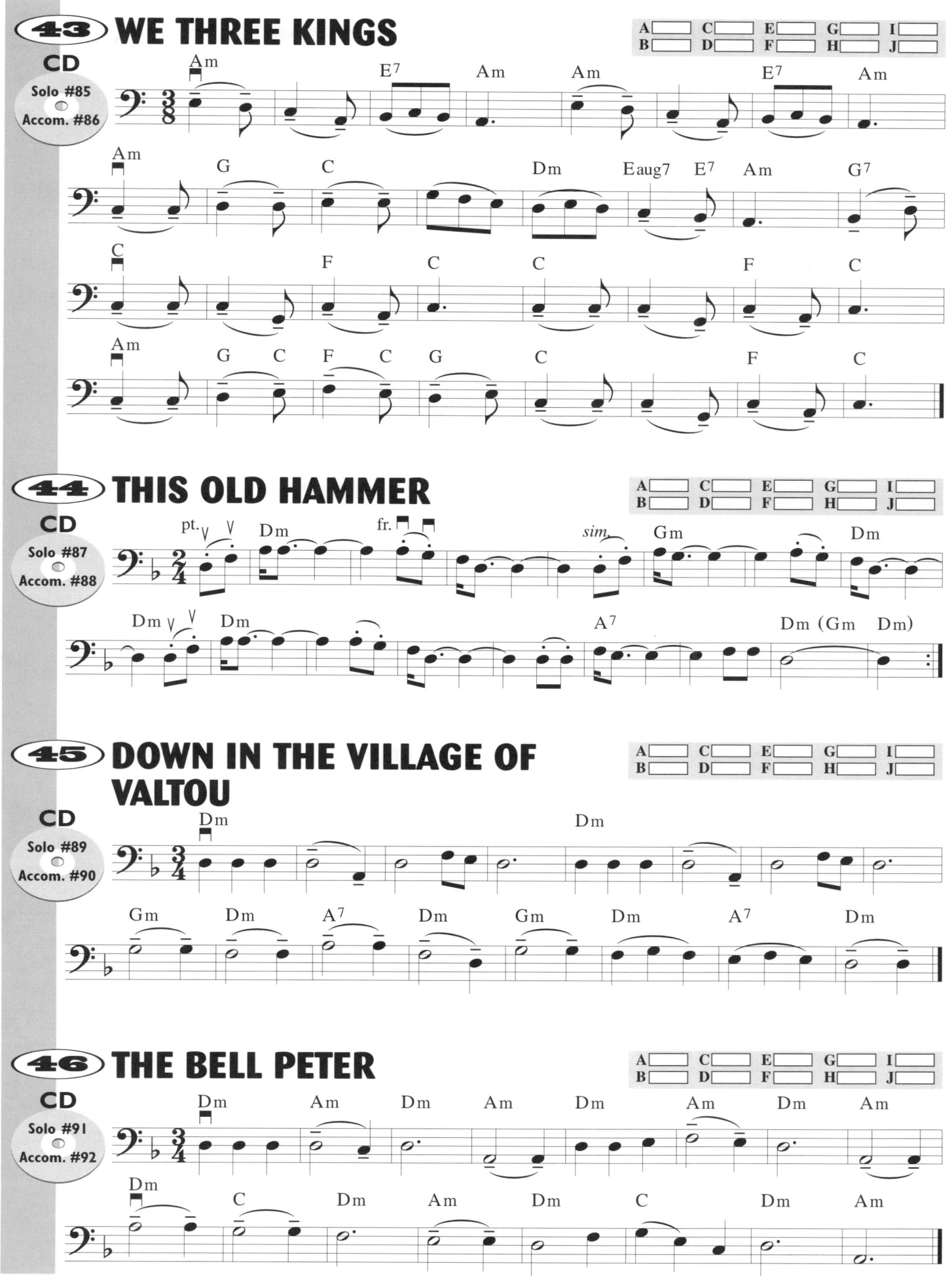